# Shades
## of Romance

Daniel Richmond

# DEDICATION

*To the lover within,*
*Who gives his heart,*
*And breaks the chains,*
*That bind the love.*

# TABLE OF CONTENTS

# ⟡ Shades of Romance

# SHADES OF ROMANCE

*I lost myself in you...*
*then lost you within myself...*

## Memories

I wish I could derive these thoughts,
from memories of hearts once crossed,
as love our feelings begins to reinvent,
emerging from the roots of our intent.

But thoughts of love are rare these days,
and my last memory so quickly fades,
it left a shadow of who I once had been,
and echoes of joy deep beneath the skin.

So deep beneath the yearning falls asleep,
not feeling and not knowing how to keep,
it rests, it thinks, it dreams of times to be,
and just as I, it longs and fights to be free.

Now disguised as heaven's sweetest rose,
an expression of beauty's perfect pose,
and like a spark she comes to reappear,
lighting this pure yearning I hold so dear.

# Oceans' Depths

I've used all kinds of sedatives,
and ways to keep you off my mind,
I've even tried the oceans' depths,
to drown this constant ticking wind.

Hoping one day someone will sear,
repressed and hidden obvious truth,
it's always you my feelings fear,
even as pain matures this youth.

And love will travel far and out,
but always stay within our reach,
a fire of words may devils shout,
if there's a lesson the heavens teach.

If God has plans we cannot see,
keeping us close for one good reason,
but if we never get to be,
can one charge God with treason?

## Passing Confusion

I didn't know what love had been,
as all my sorrows became but one,
until I saw her next to him,
all now is lost, over and done.

I hadn't felt the pain of loss,
the sour venom my feelings pump,
our love became a two-faced toss,
the birds don't sing, their tree a stump.

Let me dissolve, numb me completely,
addictive damned naïve illusion,
innocent guilt of loving freely,
adding to this passing confusion.

I love her still, and more I know,
that minds can't think what lovers feel,
she's now a breeze whose clever freeze,
makes every tear seem so unreal.

# A Path of Tears

A path of tears and broken dreams,
and sorrows crying out for rescue,
the image of a once-loved queen,
is now the memory of love's virtue.

Her true disguise is perfect beauty,
which hides all essence of her being,
yet once discovered becomes your duty,
your only reason and heart's new dealing.

And everything ends in her eyes,
those still sapphires that almost speak,
upon their light all solitude dies,
and born a wish as love's new peak.

As faith and sanity long depart,
she is the union of their two ways,
the hidden labyrinth back to your heart,
and new emotions that fill your days.

# Love Denied

Thoughts too sad and love denied,
covered me like a steel glove,
I'd seen beauty that shone inside,
then flew away this precious dove.

And ran the rivers of my desire,
flooding this long-deserted path,
what had begun to burn with fire,
had quickly dimmed into a spark.

So she became a distant dream,
that I could sleep through all my life,
a rush of joy, a soundless scream,
the reason for my lonesome strife.

But angels heard my thoughts of her,
the cries that I could not contain,
and many yearning days later,
I hear her soothing voice again.

# Untouched

The tree of beauty stands untouched,
its leaves fall dead upon de ground,
as eternity withers its branches in the sun,
and the axe of man eats away its limbs.

Firm and its beauty always untouched,
it's filled with life and nourishing light,
it hears the call for love and cries of pain,
and smiles brightly at the magic of it all.

And dear, your lips may not feel my lips,
yet I am kissing you tenderly every day,
and as I stop to think of times that were,
the call of love keeps entering these veins.

Your hands are not resting upon mine,
yet the same peaceful tenderness pervades,
and as we reach to new life, to new heights,
there is a higher touch our hearts await

# Clouded Thoughts

A woman seen that fills my life,
a girl no longer here to chase,
ideal mother and treasured wife,
the sensual goddess my feelings face.

All one with me yet so apart,
lost emptiness that yearns to find,
a rain filled river divides my heart,
as clouded thoughts still march in line.

And stepping forward causes much pain,
a measured move with strings attached,
I cannot speak such words in vain,
am I to drop these dreams far-fetched?

What would contain such overflow,
there are no chains to hold me back,
who would replace her perfect glow,
when she provides meaning I lack.

# Nine Moons

Two moons before last night,
I heard you sing again,
and as the sun was rising,
silent birds felt love's pain.

Three other moons have passed,
since laughter filled your heart,
and seeing you so glad,
gave my own a jump start.

Four moons returned at last,
your body still on earth,
divinity came down the day,
a woman gave you birth.

Nine moons summed up in all,
are what you shared with me,
let darkness fill the skies,
so moons are always seen.

# True Existence

In a forest burning of reason and dead wood,
the twinkling light of weakened hope,
which symbolizes all that is good,
cuts through that thick nostalgic smoke.

Inside this carcass full of pale bones,
ten thousand heroes scream for help,
and deeply buried in borrowed stones,
remain unheard and slowly melt.

But love so humbly marches in,
with tender armor and feathered swords,
so unintended our deepest yearning,
dissolves with tears, unspoken words.

Let eager roots from heaven's wisdom,
dance through the earth of all resistance,
and trees of hope again rise freely,
where man shall find his true existence.

# Labyrinth

The true potential of being lost,
all explained when later found,
and that long journey left to explore,
so full of thorns and rusted crowns.

Yet crumbs of hope keep us alive,
and by surprise when good luck calls,
courageously we take that dive,
and find new light as darkness falls.

Like patient sun rays that view the sea,
our curious eyes unwrap this world,
and see by will all you can be,
upon experience so quickly hurled.

So find that love which life consumes,
taking a deeper look inside,
in harshest winters your dessert blooms,
and in your heart all does abide.

# Walk Alone

How much can I carry in this heart?
can I hold the distance and the spaces,
a moment of confusion and desperation,
the love above all circumstances.

Can all these feelings be embraced?
and still leave room for that old me,
who looked with wonder at this world,
and searched for all that it could be.

What becomes when all is left behind?
when something shifts so deep inside,
as tables turn and moments redefined,
before our very eyes two worlds collide.

Questions that create so many mazes,
and some feared point of no return,
yet by your side, dear heart, I walk alone,
and let this wild inspiration burn.

*Open the doors of this heart...*
*let me answer the call of love...*

# A Kind of Beauty

The kind of beauty that dances still,
so proud to be what true men seek,
in awe, all stunned unable to speak,
and forced to fight against love's will.

Her stride livened by those long legs,
and steps that write across the ground,
leaving love's psalms without a sound,
the air around is shred to threads.

And when she stops all else stops too,
yet her reflection moves like a flame,
burning desire that leaves no shame,
what I would do to be with you.

From curves to eyes to perfect lips,
seamless sculpture and tailored descent,
what more could heaven represent,
if here on earth this angel lives.

# Bloomed with Light

Bloomed with light winter's rose,
to show her beauty once again,
as if magically transposed,
from the dreams of yearning men.

Caressed the timid wings of love,
with hidden wishes to let it fly,
like a fearless new born dove,
into the undiscovered open sky.

And all that stillness in her eyes,
contains whispers of dwindling tears,
of her encounter with other lives,
yet every day new life appears.

Now let the love inside her bloom,
so with a rose from my own heart,
I can caress her distant dreams,
and put an end to winter's start.

# Perfect Resistance

Perfection came down upon,
the day you entered my life,
and as hard as it is to maintain,
you are still its envied strife.

Resistance followed this foe,
all the way to our resting point,
saved us from the sweetest sins,
helping souls remain closely joined.

Beauty still continues to arrive,
with every word and every touch,
let those gates dissolve at once,
clearing your path, welcomed much.

Nothing more can change this past,
it is a portrait painted and dried,
where true dreams shall cast,
and tears of former lovers cried.

# Past Perfect

I've seen that perfect one,
she came to me one dawn,
the leaves had dress the earth,
that lovely day in autumn.

Her eyes were one with mine,
a shrine that shares the light,
I saw myself aside this being,
to fight with all my might.

Yet as this princess came,
I felt you from behind,
the one who lives in dreams,
and shows that love is kind.

Sweet lady once again,
you flood me with your touch,
your image hurts to see,
past perfect is not much.

# Crystal Light

Her beauty is more than crystal light,
A shining image that lures the eye,
she sits above what one can see,
divine warmth she brings to me.

And if the deaf could only hear,
her gifted voice can shed a tear,
and if the blind could only see,
as all her love can let life be.

Why must this lady be so true,
oh in my dreams what I would do,
yet in my mind nothing can match,
this ecstasy that pairs her touch.

I pray to God that her image,
were just exclusive to my eyes,
to keep her sacred from the rest,
and with her love conclude my quest.

# Simple Rhymes

Let me try just one more time,
with clear words and simple rhymes,
using sensations that crowd my spine,
what now she is through future times.

More than dreams the mind creates,
and deepest love the heart desires,
she's fertile light that life initiates,
and even more her voice inspires.

Her lyrical footprints across the sky,
stepping in front as you surrender,
your body is sand, so hard and dry,
and she like water making you tender.

And once again my words aren't much,
affirming truths these lines express,
I wish you sight, hearing and touch,
so you become my grateful witness.

# Purely Transparent

Purely transparent and so sincere,
accepting all that life has to speak,
with open arms and a voice so clear,
she'll make you feel so truly unique.

A dedicated soul devoted to love,
searching for answers in places unknown,
and picking up gladly as if sent by God,
the pieces of dreams winds have blown.

Completely embracing all of her world,
like waters so vast that make up the sea,
in a deepest abyss she has twirled,
oceans have pearls as she has beauty.

When love is the goal there's no sacrifice,
She'll quickly renounce to all that surrounds,
yet having you close is her only vice,
a drum in her heart eternally pounds.

# Sweetest Rose

The sweetest rose with thorns of steel,
covered in petals of aspiration,
a definition of love's appeal,
that lacks its rival's best imitation.

And blooming still through empathy,
a virgin that conceives with ease,
resisting sighs of actuality,
like melting ice that waits its freeze.

My thoughts alone she travels to,
with open arms like open hearts,
and so eagerly wrapped through,
turning our love into an art.

The purest love my body breathes,
so tenderly bringing me shelter,
this rose produced eternal wreaths,
that crown my agony's cooled welter.

# Impatient Walk

Seduced by time's impatient walk,
I sit and wait along this shore,
the water's flow feels dry as chalk,
and to this day seems so obscure.

The hardened pieces fall apart,
and stick like lips to this old heart,
a voice unheard that reaches far,
from deep below to my love's star.

This soul is bearing too much a weight,
a faceless soul mate in every route,
such distant heart that knows its fate,
as marching sorrows so proudly shout.

My eyes did witness such pure grace,
as heavens cloud to shed some rain,
and of those drops that fall from space,
you're still the one, my beauty stain.

# Tones of Grey

A distant dove with angel wings,
so quietly has passed me by,
the ground became a bed of springs,
watching her fly across the sky.

I could not speak a single phrase,
intimidated by such great view,
a perfect picture became her face,
and patiently I await my cue.

In fantasies my closed eyes see,
she gives new form to lustful dreams,
and drop by drop creates in me,
an overflow that true love deems.

So from afar the distance shrunk,
and closeness slowly paced our way,
the air between us squeezed aside,
as sadness colored its tones of grey.

# Whispers Unheard

Whispers in the ears of destiny,
mention her name with admiration,
a voice unheard, a face never seen,
my deepest form of inspiration.

A beauty perfected by human eyes,
that is the cruelest to the blind,
and soothes the vain's frustrated cries,
truly an image of its own kind.

Yet lust has never stained her heart,
nor walked the garden of her joy,
virgin emotions were kept apart,
from such complexities we employ.

And only water from heaven's spring,
mirrors the purity of her free spirit,
with a sincerity of life's beginning,
which passing saints shall soon inherit.

*May this instant last forever...*
*and may forever heal this past...*

# The Sun Rises

The sun rises and she is next to me,
what a pleasant way to start this day,
all wrapped in sheets, our bodies free,
triggered by touch, there is no other way.

We cool our magnetized and heated lust,
our love makes every road so viable,
the space between, gone with a thrust,
and every look we give so tangible.

Like knots one would tie to save a life,
our bodies joined seem only one,
and still our eyes the star's device,
as fortune bounces off the sun.

Drops of sweat like curtains help us rest,
we're still in love after our friendly fight,
my warrior, she's still all beauty's best,
a conquest of self-rendered might.

# This Morning

My dear and sweet Beloved,
this morning my soul communes with You,
like waters merging back together,
as the ship of separation passes through.

Light begins to enter this silent room,
the sun's brilliant rays cover me entirely,
they closely resemble the fullness of your heart,
which keeps me alive and present so blissfully.

My eyes close again as they did in the night,
an image, like a radiant portrait, fills my mind,
Your beauty within redefines beauty without,
and I feel your touch, so pleasant and kind.

This is how the day begins for me,
I lay in wonder beneath the greatness of the sky,
Love is the Divinity that sees through all of life,
And You, my Love, are the mirror in its eye.

.

# Drop of Sorrow

In the rain of undiscovered beauty,
a drop of sorrow has found its place,
descended so silently upon me,
and its reflection revealed her face.

The darkest silk atop brown sapphires,
and skin that speaks the hymn of lust,
dresses the curves of my desires,
as breaths comprise their wishful gust.

Her voice resounds in all of space,
reveals such great kaleidoscope,
of innocence, curiosity and grace,
and this heart feels a new born hope.

In the presence of tamed seduction,
patience became our closest friend,
like the pleasant dance of interaction,
between two souls that slowly mend.

# Effortless

For as long as I can remember,
the wind had not cooled my face,
nor had beauty warmed my heart,
with such eloquent effortless grace.

And it's that beauty that stands alone,
undressed yet covered with purity,
it has your eyes, your skin and touch,
and through your voice resounds in me.

Like answered prayers it reappears,
to be the fire beneath my dreams,
and the momentum of my desire,
so love no longer is what it seems.

It is your image that multiplies,
in the yearning mind of every man,
and every fool that let you pass by,
whose hope ended where mine began.

# Eager Mouths

The words I find are not enough,
and those which were not spoken yet,
by hungry hearts through eager mouths,
still can't describe this love we whet.

A love as pure as angels' faith,
and as impulsive as faithless spurs,
by all that lives inside these veins,
I'd give my life so it remains.

To speak her name resounds above,
those prayers which God will only hear,
with his creation to share his love,
and keep my heart's desire sincere.

Before we part one final time,
my deepest wish that she be mine,
a yearning's truth has lost its shine,
from God to me, from blood to wine.

# Sweet Caress

To experience your sweet caress,
the serenity your beauty emanates,
ignites a wild fire I must suppress,
until peace once again resonates.

Yet mighty sparks break through,
away from fears of further pain,
they keep this love undeniably true,
and let our hearts closely remain.

As calm silence fills my thought,
only the image of your face exists,
and the memories our lives brought,
like undefeatable warriors persist.

I'd cross an ocean of endless strife,
to feel your breath against my lips,
and whether friend, lover or wife,
our souls will form the same eclipse.

# Before Her

Before her, truest beauty had no rival,
and the sun was still the brightest star,
in that space crucial to love's survival,
her essence is a whisper heard afar.

That innocent touch confuses reality,
since dreams also do carry such grace,
as silence crowds the edges of sanity,
light reshapes to the image of her face.

An alliance of perfection and desire,
rules the surroundings of every word,
born of virgin lips armed with such fire,
and reaches like purity's flying bird.

Let that whisper, that fire, that beauty,
experience the freedom of the untamed,
and every moment relieved of all duty,
beyond feelings that remain unnamed.

# Patient Soul

A patient soul unknown to sin,
goes as red and slowly enters,
but as the night unfolds its fins,
the red turns blue, her eyes unshelter.

She is so silent in her expression,
yet expresses all there is to know,
the dance of invisible attraction,
awaits the symphonies of her glow.

And with a simple blink of sight,
all her beauty comes shining through,
with unsurpassable eager might,
only attainable by fortune's few.

A thin line between lust and shyness,
she paces with her heart so closed,
and walks the world whose blindness,
has left her solitude exposed.

# Comfortably Afraid

I didn't know what love could do,
my heart gave up that treacherous quest,
all I know is I fell in love with you,
and sounds of joy beat upon my chest.

But I grew comfortable and afraid,
and from our deepest nature strayed,
for fear and comfort go hand in hand,
and leave this love without command.

The cautious heart that plans its fate,
neglects to see a love so great,
that knows no fear and treads with ease,
and finds itself back on its knees.

I pray to feel you ever more,
and crack you open from the core,
so that I too can see what's true,
and free this love that burns for you.

# A Dreamer's Life

A dreamer's life is not her own,
but of the valiant dreams she weaves,
and as her heart turns every stone,
the world becomes what she believes.

Knitted with love are all her words,
clear as the sky her vision of peace,
in chilling turmoil her light brings warmth,
and rooted in wisdom she treads with ease.

Devoted and surrendered she knows no fear,
for nothing is lost when all is given,
unguarded, untethered all pain disappears,
all pages turned and all debts forgiven.

This life indeed is not her own,
but of the loving will that she portrays,
and as her heart and mind atone,
she holds the world with brilliant rays.

# Naked Hearts

Empty moments have flooded the darkest night,
as the eve of solitude sheltered our separation,
but now rain pours through a brilliant light,
so kiss me wildly and without restriction.

Join these naked hearts and hungry hands,
in the purest music of freedom and adventure,
as our eager feet follow this precious dance,
and witness with wonder our past's departure.

Walk with me and gently leave behind,
the shadows of any unfulfilled expectation,
and let that sweet silence help us to remind,
of who we truly are and the fruits of liberation.

Break the chains around these scripted words,
and let our tongues express and deeply feel,
while we join each other like two fearless birds,
that fly so freely as they love, mend and heal.

*Within my own unguarded heart...*
*Love showed herself again...*

# A Little Time

I will need a little time,
to be the man you yearn to find,
to find in me the strength to fly,
to stop the clock that shakes my heart,
to push this world, this loaded cart,
to show a heart that loves to feel,
to give you love that feels so real,
to see above the perfect blue,
and wake in bed aside of you.

# Desire in My Heart

Greetings again desire in my heart,
enabler of dreams,
of deep emotions and things to come.

My dear old mate,
who watched me grow from pain to Love,
and stood by me through darkest nights,
to be the friend I never had.

I see you here in front of me,
with your intentions to set me free,
and therefore, I bow to you,
for seeing through,
for not relying on what seems real,
but on what hearts can feel as True.

# Love is a Gift

If love were just a gift,
that one could find and give,
I'd walk the world in bare feet,
and swim through oceans' endless deep,
in search of you... the love to keep.

If love were simply smiles,
that flow to touch and end in bed,
I'd make you laugh from toe to head,
and let your skin and my hands wed,
to let us rest... our hungers fed.

If love were only names,
that come across this endless life,
I'd joyfully repeat yours twice,
and let dissolve this lonesome strife,
my only love... sweet sacrifice.

# Wandering Man

Deep into an arctic forest,
that once flourished,
as a jungle of love,
arrived a new message,
by tired old wings,
of a traveling dove.

"Be ever so present,
in your moments of bliss,
be ever so tender,
when receiving love's kiss".

Not so easily read,
had been written by hand,
by the feverish wishes,
of a trembling man.

Had they been final words?
at the time of his death,
was he sharing his sorrows,
as he took that last breath?

Many years now passed,
since the note was flown in,
and the winters grew warmer,
than they ever had been.

Yet today in the fields,
where sweet rivers now ran,
lies there still the soft echo,
of that wandering man.

# Bedrock of Love

The enticing allure of beauty and lust,
for a thirsty heart this how it begins,
there is nothing to question or even to trust,
just the pleasure of tasting the sweetest sins.

Then in the distance a reflection light,
appearing in the silence of a quiet mind,
like a flame of hope in the vast dark night,
brings warmth to the heart and sight to the blind.

A love beyond vision and free of conditions,
only purity of feeling and being alive,
and what once was a nest of vibrant suspicions,
is the bedrock of truth where we've longed to arrive.

# Many Places

I've looked for God in many places,
in different faces,
and feelings high and low,
through love that turned to lust,
dissolved into the dust,
and as my feelings turned.
I witnessed Love's return.

I've let the flame of inspiration burn,
my fears run wild,
and watched as doubt seduced my heart,
I've met with life and all its parts,
when all was joy and bliss,
or grief and pain were passing by,
and lived through endless fresh new starts.

Now I look at all that is,
at all that's ever been,
and see myself down on my knees,
where only Love and Life reside,
and evermore I long to fly,
into the sweetest mystery I dive..

# Here we Are

I see you rising,
through the bitter sweet ashes,
of a past that shouldn't have been,
and could have been,
rising even further,
I see you here and now,
rooted in the beauty,
deep beneath the skin.


Your image is vibrant,
in the mirror of the heart,
where I also see myself,
but I look behind me,
and you are vanished,
yet in that mirror,
there you are,
twice as far,

I breathe,
quenching my thirst,
again and again,
I breathe,
from the fountain of life,
from the breath of God,
and as every mirror shatters,
here we are.

# Fearless State

We begin to die,
the moment we are born,
breaking free from the womb,
from a lover,
from ourselves,
into the distance,
our hearts are torn,
cracked open,
dissolved onto existence.

Each moment passes,
and more breaths we take,
dwelling in time and space,
moving in cycles,
confused and diffused,
in a circular tent,
for our body's sake,
a circus of memories,
smiling in the lion's den.

But Love is rediscovered,
and death is born again,
mortality surrenders itself,
its concern and dominance,
its cry for help,
and pleasing traits,
without the pain,
life's beautiful essence,
in a fearless state.

## Two Hearts

When two hearts meet,
and lover's palms unite,
the air becomes so sweet,
and passion's flames ignite.

We're stripped of any reason,
and very deep inside,
can feel a change of season,
as yearning hearts collide.

Our eyes then share one light,
reflecting one same love,
and ecstasy takes flight,
like freedom's blissful dove.

There is no guilt or sin,
there is no you or I,
no "fool who let you in"
and doubts begin to die.

We feel that subtle breeze,
from which all fires feed,
it brings us to our knees,
and meets our every need.

This is the prize to claim,
at once when two hearts meet,
the real and lasting flame,
which lover's share and keep.

So let this wind carry you,
as it blows no one knows,
where it came from,
where it goes.

# Into Your Arms I Die

Within each day,
I live my whole life,
in darkness I arise,
not even the moon shines,
in silence and solitude,
I look for you again,
and there you are.

The sun rises,
a life begins within a day,
I see all that I am,
beyond time and mind,
beyond sorrow and pain,
fear, doubt and shame,
in falling I rise up,
cleaning the slate,
climbing and striving,
within myself,
the search is never ending.

In looking I remember,
amnesia of the past,
discarding an old self,
a self I never was,
crumbs of joy,
a glimpse of total bliss,
then vanished I become.

The sun moves through me,
from top to bottom,
from left to right,
all within this day,
this life,
love and celebration,
the Joy of who I am,
all that I am.

The moon slowly enters,
it greets me in the night,
in peace I lay to rest,
and once again,
into your arms,
I die.

# ABOUT
## THE AUTHOR

**Daniel Richmond's** collection of poems reveals the restlessness of the seeker, the sensitivity of the lover, the pain that comes with depth, and leaves with depth, the agility and sharpness of the intellect woven through the gentleness of the soul and the heart. Like their author, the poems are beautifully open and honest, yet keeping the essential mystery of the human quest for meaning, clarity and love.

Each poem has its own unmistakable identity clearly defined and guiding the reader through a journey, a dance choreographed by a firm but light hand.

Like a painter, Daniel sets about with primary colors and then washes them into subtle shades while keeping the core, the strongest theme, the seeking. The poems are his search for clear answers, gentleness and wonder.

Daniel is a profoundly gentle yet strong soul, with a great desire for an absolute purity of love. His quest is apparent, heart focused as well as heart rendering.

To read more of Daniel
Richmond's latest work visit
**www.danielrichmond.com**

www.ingramcontent.com/pod-product-compliance
Lightning Source LLC
Chambersburg PA
CBHW021134020426
42331CB00005B/771